New Zealand:

100% pure

Vincenzo Berghella

Copyright Page

Copyright year: 2014

ISBN No: 978-0-578-14245-6

From the same author:

- **Obstetric Evidence Based Guidelines.** Informa Healthcare, London, UK, and New York, USA (2007) [English]

- **Maternal Fetal Evidence Based Guidelines.** Informa Healthcare, London, UK, and New York, USA (2007) [English]

- **Laughter, the best medicine. Jokes for everyone.** (2007) [English]

- **Ridere, la migliore medicina. Barzellette per bambini.** (2007) [Italiano]

- **My favorite quotes.** (2009) [English]

- **In medio stat virtus – Citazioni d'autore.** (2009) [Italiano]

- **Quello che di voi vive in me.** (2009) [Italiano]

- **Dall'altra parte dell'oceano.** (2010) [Italiano] [Translated in: **On the other side of the ocean.** (2013) [English]

- **Preterm Birth: Prevention and Management.** Wiley-Blackwell. Oxford, United Kingdom. (2010) [English]

- **From father to son.** (2010) [English]

- **Sollazzi.** (2010) [Italiano]

- **The land of religions.** (2011) [English] [Translated in: **La terra delle religioni.** (2013) [Italiano]

- **Giramondo.** (2011) [Italiano]

- **Obstetric Evidence Based Guidelines.** Informa Healthcare, London, UK, and New York, USA (2012; Second Edition) [English]

- **Maternal Fetal Evidence Based Guidelines.** Informa Healthcare, London, UK, and New York, USA (2012; Second Edition) [English]

- **Trip to London.** (2012) [English]

- **Il primo amore non si scorda mai**. (2012) [Italiano]

- **Maldives.** (2013) [English]

- **Russia.** (2013) [English]

- **Happiness: the scientific path to achieving well-being** (2014) [English]

Pre-travel excitement

I've been wishing to go to New Zealand all my life. It must have been in middle school, in Italy, that a geography teacher told us that New Zealand was on the other side of the world from where we were. She said that if we made a hole below us all the way to the other side, we would find ourselves in New Zealand.

In fact, she made us look at the globe. She even pointed out that New Zealand was on the opposite side of the equator. Italy in the Northern hemisphere, New Zealand in the Southern. New Zealand's shape also resembles Italy's, but upside down, missing Italy's north part, on top of the boot.

Growing up, my childhood fascination has continued. The Southern Hemisphere is where one can see the Southern sky. In high school the beachfront I went to with friends in my home town of Pescara, on the Eastern Adriatic shore of Central Italy, was called 'Croce del Sud,' or 'Southern Cross.' My rugby friends were passionate about the All Blacks, New Zealand's famed national rugby team, often seemingly unbeatable. Growing up on the shore, I always followed the America's Cup, the biggest and most prestigious sailing race in the world. Seeing New Zealanders take this trophy away from the perennial American powerhouse winners was impressive.

This year I turned 50. Last year, for Paola's celebrations, we all went to the Maldives, a dream destination for beach, sun, and relaxation (even if she agreed to Club Med and lots of activities on those fabled islands). This year it is up to me to choose. The choice is relatively easy. Paola and I have now taken the kids, apart from their native North America, to other 4 continents, including South America, Europe, Africa, and Asia. Given we all don't have much desire to go to Antarctica, the only continent left is Oceania.

I do get some push back initially from Paola. Too far, not cultured enough, what are the kids going to learn, etc. But last year she chose the Maldives, so some of these arguments are not so strong. We do have only a week, which would possibly make this a bit of a rush, and she is absolutely right about that. But we are good at compromising, and our conversations for the vast part improve our common decisions.

We agree to go just to the South Island, where I heard the best and most adventurous sites of New Zealand are located. What I think really turns the match in my favor is my proposal (thanks to our friend Paolo's suggestion) to do the sightseeing via camper. Paola and I have always fantasized about doing a trip with the kids on an RV (Recreational Vehicle, what a wonderful name). Now we find the right opportunity. My efforts to get everybody else as galvanized as I was beginning to work.

As a pre-teen, I remember looking mesmerized at the beautiful round globe that my grandfather Vincenzo had in his home office. It was old, and, in the middle of the Pacific Ocean, you could run your finger, from North to South Pole, on the little ridge formed by the just-a-position of the paper edges coming from East and West. One could palpate the scotch tape which kept the two parts of the world united.

And it is exactly along this raised, palpable border that time inexplicably changes. Not just an hour, as in other time zones. Here, along this long vertical ridge, the date on one side is different than the date on the other side. It was hard for me so young to comprehend this concept. It is still hard, even now.

So on the morning before our departure, to begin to animate our two sons Andrea and Pietro, I ask what they are planning to do March 23, 2014. Their faces are puzzled. Then I tell Andrea he could finally answer as he always does when I ask him about his day after school or when I pick him up from an after school sporting event. "Nothing," he usually says.

But this time he would be right, I tell him. March 23, 2014 will not exist for us. We'll board a plane on March 22nd at 7pm in Los Angeles. Twelve hours later, we'll land in Auckland, New Zealand, were the time will be 7am, but of March 24th, 2014!!

As in any trip, I've studied a few books and tour guides in preparation. I have discovered recently, taking a Gallup Personality test, that my number one Strength is 'Learner.' I just love to study, and acquire knowledge. New Zealand is a wonderful subject, on which I do not know much, but which has always fascinated me.

New Zealand is one of the youngest landmasses on our planet. Moreover, New Zealand is the last land mass to be discovered. It has been populated with humans for less than eleven centuries. Sailors probably from Polynesia, in particular from Tahiti, colonized these two islands. Physical traits and language of the Maori, who are New Zealand's original inhabitants, are closely related to Tahiti, 2,698 miles (or 4,342 kilometers) to the North-East of Oceania.

The best estimates are that in 925 CE, Kupe sailed from Hawaiki and discovered New Zealand. He called it *Aoteroa*, or the Land of the Long White Cloud. In 1350 CE, eight war canoes landed in Aoteroa, and began Maori civilization. Of course, there is a Maori legend on how New Zealand was really formed. The demigod Maui sailed on a canoe from Hawaiki, probably a French Polynesian island, and caught a huge fish, which he dragged to the surface. The fish is the North Island. Maui's canoe is the South Island.

In 1642, the Dutch captain Abel Tasman sighted the South Island, but never set foot on it, as he was attacked by the Maori. Captain Cook arrived in the Bay of Islands, in New Zealand's North Island, in 1769, the first time a 'civilized' man from the West set foot on this land. Later that century whalers and sealers arrived, started colonization, and introduced diseases and firearms. Missionaries arrived in the 1800s, bringing Christianity and farming.

In 1840, on February 6th, the Maori and the British signed the Treaty of Waitangi. The Treaty guaranteed Maori rights to the land, but it gave the British sovereignty. The New Zealand's capital was moved from Russell in the bay of islands to Auckland, where it remained for 25 years. But violent land wars between Maori and British eventually continued. In 1865 Wellington was made the capital, which it still is today.

New Zealand is very much a former British colony. Kiwis – as New Zealanders are often called - speak English, and drive on the left side of the road. Given that I was going to drive, for the first time, a 6.6 meter long RV, it would certainly be an adventure. The food is mostly meat and vegetables, with plenty of salty pies and typical British fare. They are light skinned, with many blondes, and lots of blue eyes. Surprisingly, they use the metric system instead of pounds and miles.

New Zealand went on to be the first country to legalize unions in 1878, and the first to give women the vote, a wonderful achievement they should be very proud of. Despite being not a large country and far away from the battlefields of the two World Wars, New Zealand and many of its people participated in both, with heavy casualties.

In 1953, local boy Edmund Hillary with sherpa Tensing Norgay climbed Everest. More recently, in October of 2011, the All Blacks won again the Rugby World Cup. I remember watching it, tipped about it by my good French friend Olivier, whose country was beaten that day by the national rugby team that has a over 75% winning record.

As one can tell by this very brief recount, New Zealand does not have much history. It does not have the millennial cultural roots and traditions of the Middle East, Egypt, Greece or Rome. But its 1,000-mile long land has nearly every environment on the planet, from glaciers to volcanoes, from beaches to forests. About one third of New Zealand, or more than five million acres, are protected in parks and reserves. Tourism is New Zealand's second industry, after agriculture. New Zealanders like to call their country '100% pure.' This is their strength and trademark.

The South Island is the stunner, with the highest mountain in Oceania (Aoraki/Mt Cook, at 12,316 feet), Fiordland National Park, raw wilderness and wild weather. Hillary practiced at Mt Cook before successfully climbing Everest. I plan for us to see at least four of the places in New Zealand listed in the '1,000 places to see before you die' book: Arthur's Pass, Aoraki, Fiordland National Park, and Queenstown. Kiwis, as New Zealanders are referred to from their national bird, love the outdoors, which here are beautiful.

I can't wait to do the best New Zealand tourist's activities, according to what the few friends who have been there and the travel guide books I started to read say. Off road driving, rafting, mountain biking and cycling, kayaking, sailing, boat cruising, diving, white water rafting, jet boating, paragliding. Bungy jumping, invented in the South Island, is the only activity I am planning on skipping.

Saturday March 22

The first flight is USAir 783, leaving Philadelphia at 4:05pm. We first feast on original, almond, and cinnamon Aunt Anne's pretzels. Delicious. Our four (one each) carry-ons are all allowed on, while we cannot yet change our seats, which are scattered throughout the plane, on the next flight, also a Star Alliance flight. On this first flight we have good seats, 17A, 17B, 16A, 16B, so Paola and I are just in front of Pietro and Andrea. I take a few photos of them as they are laughing behind us. They are the best of pals. Inseparable, never fighting, always looking for each other. I hope and trust they'll stay like this all their lives.

The weather is good throughout our ride, but there is no in flight entertainment. So it feels a bit long, after reading and writing for four hours straight I get a bit bored. Andrea plays with his games on the iPhone, Pietro plays solitaires games with cards and reads his book a bit. We arrive in Los Angeles at 7:11pm, after about 6 hours of flying.

In Los Angeles sunset has just occurred, so it's dark outside. We have about a three-hour layover. We have to go to Baggage Claim and go from Terminal 3 where we landed to Terminal 2, from where our flight to Auckland will take off. Here Muhammad, the Air New Zealand staff at check-in, is strict. He has us weigh our carry-ons, and each is over 7kg, the weigh limit to take them on board. They are each about 11kg. I even try to take the laptop out to get closer to within limits, but to no avail. We have only a one hour and forty-five minute layover in Auckland, so we are a bit worried that having to go through international customs in Auckland and then retrieve our carry-ons will make us loose our connection to Christchurch.

We beg Muhammad. We are silver members of Star Alliance. "Please at least check the luggage all the way to Christchurch, so we can skip baggage claim and have a higher chance of making the next flight." He does not budge. He says that, while both flights are Air New Zealand, they have been booked with separate reservations, so he cannot do anything about the luggage.

I remember when, going to Lima, Peru, from Philadelphia, via three different flights, we also were not allowed to take carry-ons with us. I was livid then, but here I'm more relaxed; I have to adjust and keep cool, I've tried everything I can, I certainly am not going to ask for a supervisor, I never do, and this guy is just doing his job. Later in Auckland I'll confirm with another agent that Muhammad in Los Angeles was indeed just following the rules.

Having to look into my luggage to try to come within weigh limits, I realize that I do not have my new Kindle, which is traveling with me for the first time, in my trolley or my backpack. I must have left it on the plane from Philadelphia to Los Angeles. We decide to split: Pietro Andrea and Paola will go on and pass customs at Terminal 2, while I'll go back to Terminal 3 to try to retrieve it.

I first ask the US Airways check-in counter, where an agent is super-kind, and calls by walkie-talkie the staff person who is already cleaning the plane. After waiting politely about five minutes on the side, he hears back and then tells me that the cleaning crew has not found anything extra in seats 16 A, B, and C, where Paola and I had sprawled. He advises me to report this to US Airways Baggage office, which is just downstairs. I do, finding another kind gentleman to take my info. I accept I've lost the Kindle, it's just all my fault, about $100 lost, but there are a lot worst things in life.

Once I walk back to Terminal 2, the staff lets me go in the much shorter check-in line as a silver member for Star Alliance, and so I join Paola Andrea and Pietro relatively quickly after they themselves have gotten through. We find the right gate, and, as planned, sit down in a restaurant nearby to have dinner around 9pm. They have three hamburgers, I have a tuna melt. Tradition respected.

At 10:15pm Air New Zealand flight number 1 from Los Angeles to Auckland seems to be on time. A sea of people is waiting to board it. We realize that also Air New Zealand flight number 5 is leaving from Los Angeles to Auckland, but at 11pm. That is why so many are waiting at the huge gate number 23. We have seats 45F, 46F, 55J, and 55F.

Despite my much trying both online and by calling Air New Zealand, I had not been able to get us seats together. We had even asked Muhammad earlier, but all he said he could do, is call the gate and tell the staff about our request. Hearing how he had done this and the pronunciation of our last names had left in me little hope of success in getting better seats. Again, I had had little faith. At the gate, they say they knew we had requested better seats, so they have ready, already printed, four brand new tickets for 38 D through F, four middle seats all together! Happiness.

As we wait to board, Andrea looks everywhere for a plug where to recharge his iPhone. He finally finds one. They board initially first class rows 1-12, then business 12-31, then economy from the back, all the way from rows in the 60s. We, in row 38, are the last group to board, which is just fine as we have only small backpacks.

The line-up is, from right to left, Pietro, Andrea, Paola, and Vincenzo. The seats are comfortable, the food edible. Pietro complains of some toothache, and Paola gives him some ibuprofen. He forgot to bring his retainer to his recent trip to the Portorico, so we attribute the pain so his teeth realigning. There are over a hundred movies to watch. I watch the first half hour of the Whale Rider, then sleep almost eight hours, then finish watching it. It is a great movie, filmed in New Zealand. Pietro watches Borat and other movies, and sleeps the least, probably only three or four hours.

Monday March 24

In Auckland we have to go to Baggage Claim (here called Baggage Reclaim), get our luggage which comes out quickly given it's tagged 'Priority,' and go from Terminal 3 where we landed to Terminal 2, which is the Domestic terminal. We call home, first Viterbo and my in-laws. I joke saying they do not know what time or day it is, because they say it's 8:30pm in the evening on Sunday, and I say it is indeed 8:30, but am and on Monday. Then I also call my parents.

In the meanwhile, I buy two chocolate muffins and two chocolate croissants, as well as a coke, for the troops. This all gets devoured in a couple of minutes. Pietro has slept little, and is also complaining of a toothache. We assume that this is probably from not having worn his tooth retainer during the six days he spent in Puerto Rico during his first week of spring break, just prior to this trip to Oceania. He must be exhausted.

We board Air New Zealand flight 509 from Auckland – in the North Island - to Christchurch –in the South Island - from terminal 28. Everything is on time. The flight is supposed to leave Auckland at 9am and arrive at Christchurch at 10:20am. We have seats 21C, 20D, 20E, 20F. Of course 21C is mine, Paola somehow always seats with the kids when we have three seats in a row in these planes. The flight time is about one hour and 4 minutes. Everyone is nice and polite. Nobody cuts in line, in fact people seem to play a game of who is more courteous.

Christchurch is called 'Garden City' because of the beautiful flora here. The original name stems from its founders. John Robert Godley was sent by a British organization, called the Canterbury Association, to prepare for the arrival of 800 settlers in the new town. He gave it the name of its college at Oxford. The town has an English quality to it, and is a little slice of England, really.

On September 4th, 2010, a magnitude 7.1 earthquake caused considerable damage here. But on February 22nd, 2011, a magnitude 6.3 aftershock, closer to the city center, caused not only massive damage but the loss of more than 180 lives.

At 350,000 inhabitants, Christchurch (or 'ChCh,' as locals call it) is the largest city in South Island, and the second largest in New Zealand, after Auckland. Interestingly, it is also the forward supply depot for the main US Antarctic base at McMurdo.

Once we arrive in Christchurch and get our luggage, I ask personnel in the terminal about directions to where the Britz Campervan counter is. They direct me to a near-by counter where we can call Britz to confirm our arrival and get picked up to go to where our campervan is. We have to dial the number '65' a few times to finally get someone on the phone. I also have the number for the Britz Christchurch branch (+64 3 357 5610).

Once I finally get a young, kind female voice on the phone, with a heavy New Zealand accent that I have obviously not mastered yet, she recognizes our reservation right away, but says we should wait for now at the airport and get some food, as they are very busy and could not get to us for over an hour.

I stand firm; we have been traveling for quite some time, I'd rather get out of the airport to wherever Britz 'temporary, cold, not-so-nice' station is. So she, reluctantly, directs us by phone to walk to a car park nearby and wait under the down ramp, where the shuttle pick up point is. Our shuttle indeed comes in five minutes. The driver has clearly been told we did not want to wait, and warns us again about the expected delay in service. It's a gorgeous upper-60's degree sunny day, and I cannot wait to stay a bit outside in fresh air.

In fact, we have quite a bit of fun now in this hour of interval at the Britz office. I ask if I can borrow a ball, which is just lying there inside a children playground. Andrea, Pietro and I play soccer on the grass. It's so beautiful outside that we sweat a bit, and end up taking our socks out, and most layers, leaving only cotton buttoned-down shirts and pants on. Delight. The decision not to stay at the airport was definitively the right one.

Paola informs us we have been called, and we receive once again courteous and comprehensive service. I sign all the paperwork. Once done, I ask the older caring woman where we can stay overnight with the RV. She gives us a large binder book on all of New Zealand's camping sites, which some other tourists had left behind. This lady is nice.

A lovely blond, blue-eyed girl takes us to the campervan, and explains how it all works. Water, water escape, gas, electricity, poop and pee repository, are just on the outside. Inside she shows us the bathroom, the kitchen, two nice tables and booths with couches, the control station with six buttons, how to turn on lights, water pump, electricity and several other instruments.

Inside we have sleeping space for six. Andrea and Pietro plan to take the top floor king bed. Paola is below them in a small queen-size bed. I'm all by myself in the rear in another small queen-size bed with a bit more leg space. We discover the helpful young girl is originally from Ireland.

The car is a diesel, with over 230,000 miles on it already. Certainly not their newest, but from the inside and outside it compares well with all the others. In fact, we initially have the impression to be just in their best campervan in a lot of over fifty, at least.

I'll have to drive on the left side of the road, which was the biggest worry of my dad. I remember when, a teenager in England, I almost got killed taking a right turn on my bike. But left-hand driving proves overall to be fairly straightforward. It's almost trickier as a pedestrian to learn to first look on the right side for incoming traffic when crossing a road. Driving here is a breeze, I love it.

The experience in the campervan, as RV is called here, is a treat in itself. Andrea, about 15 minutes into our trip, is laughing out loud in the back. He is exploding in open laughs, saying he is already having so much fun in the recreational vehicle. Yes!

Paola had me promise that our first stop would be at a supermarket. We got directions from the Britz staff for one, which proves to be only about a couple of miles out of our way. There, we buy lots of cookies, milk, cola (on sale), apples and other fruits, including a kiwiana, a local fruit. This is the size of a mango, but orangy-red on the outside, and with many pointy spots on it. As I'll do throughout the trip, I ask a local customer what it is. The friendly Kiwi says it tastes a bit like cucumber, and has an aftertaste of banana.

The cookies are on sale, so we buy four different kinds, NZ$8 (eight New Zealand dollars, which are each valued at 80 US cents currently) for each two pack combo. Chocolate chip, plain white buttery, raisins and granola, and another local kind, with one side layered with chocolate. In each of these bags, at least 30 delicious, large cookies. These will be a big highlight of the trip!

The plan agreed on by the troops is to start driving towards Arthur Pass. This is the first of the four '1,000 places to see before you die' in South Island we plan to visit, together with Mt Cook, Queenstown, and Milford Sound. In my typed tentative itinerary, I do have noted that the drive there is 153 km, estimated to take about 105min. The things to see are forest, rivers, cattle, sheep, creek, waterfalls, and wildflowers.

We look for signs for route 73 and take it. As the travel guides say, the way itself is the marvel. It is a continuous photo op. In fact, I look towards the back of the van, and see Pietro and Andrea taking pictures of the stunning landscape views. I get right from the start of this trip a great sense of family, of success.

Sheep are everywhere. New Zealand is the world's second highest producer after Australia. According to some Kiwi we meet later in our trip, New Zealand also produces all the cow milk for China: a nation of 4 million people producing enough of something for a nation of over a billion people. Sheep are not used for milk, just for their wool. Along the way, as I'll do every day, every couple of minutes I'll be shouting 'sheep,' or, less often, 'cows,' as I spot them on the way. There are over 40 million sheep in New Zealand.

We have read that Castle Hill Conservation area has interesting rock formations. Andrea spots the small signs for this site, and we do stop. There are in fact oddly shaped huge rocks up on the hill in front of us. We park the van in the large gravel parking lot, and take on a short path in the grass towards the grey large stones in front of us.

There is wild grass on the side of the path. I'm a bit tired from the long trip, and eager to connect back to earth. Plus I read on the guides (Fodor's and Lonely Planet) that there are no snakes in New Zealand. So I just lay down on the grass, happy to rest for a couple of minutes as Paola Andrea and Pietro slowly catch up with me. I look at the sky, a light blue, with few slow moving clouds. I'm happy.

Pietro Andrea and I climb up a couple of these rocks, and I do feel a bit dizzy from the trip. But I also feel alive, connected to nature. There is almost nobody else around. In the twenty minutes or so we spend at this site, probably only three or four people quietly pass by us.

I also decide to climb the small rocky hill in front of us. Andrea and Pietro see me, and follow up to where I am. Paola takes some pictures of us from below. Even just about 40 meters up, the view is spectacular, as this is a long green valley surrounded by beautiful mountains. For the most part, these are the kind of stunning views we'll see throughout our trip around the South Island.

We then take off again, and get to Arthur's Pass. While I did have some notes on what to do, I encourage the others to decide on the different possible options. Andrea in particular is into reviewing my notes, looking at the two travel guides, and helping to decide where to go. Thinking back about it, what I will most remember this trip for is the tremendous bonding of us as a family, the indelible unique memories we'll share, which will forever bring us closer.

The best option is to hike one of the three short recommended trails. Paola picks the one with the best waterfall, called Devil's trail, with **Punchbowl Falls**. We park in the gravel parking lot, with only a couple of other cars in sight.

By now it's about 4pm, it's cloudy, a bit misty, and much colder than before. As instructed by travel guides and websites, we put on more layers. I have three, the maximum I'll ever wear: a shirt (still the same from Philadelphia...), a fleece black jacket (I brought two old ones, a Nike and a NorthFace), and a grey and black NorthFace waterproof jacket. I also put on my wool black hat, and I carry with me my old black gloves.

The walk is about an hour back and forth. As Pietro rightly points out, more than a hike this is a climbing stairs path, as we step up the mountain. Everything is green. The only noise is the singing of some invisible exotic birds. Soon, after about 10 minutes, one can get a glimpse of the gorgeous waterfall. It is **140 meters (460 feet) high**.

When we get there we are the only ones on the platform, right under it. The water takes a mad free dash through the air down to the rocks in front of us. We can feel tiny water mist hit our faces. There is peace, as well as grandeur, in this natural setting.

The sign in front of the waterfall calls it Te Taunea o Hinekakai. This is clearly the Maori name. It explains that Maori associated natural features in the landscape with ancestors or their actions. Their stories linked the people to the landscape and reflected the inseparable ties between the natural and the human world.

The legend here is that, to the Ngai Tahu people, these long intertwining threads of white water from the waterfall resemble the threads of dressed flax – whitau or muka – used to weave fine garments and mats. The falls were named for an ancestress, Hinekakai, a famous weaver. She was the wife of Turakautahi, a son of Tuahuriri and the principal Tgai Tahu chief of his time, who established the Ngai Tahu stronghold at Kaiapoi. There are so many beautiful Maori stories in New Zealand, thousands of them. I plan to buy a book of them one day.

As we walk back down, I understand why they refer here often to Mother Earth and Father Sky. I pat my hand against the earth, and it feels like I'm the first one in all the history of the world to touch this moss and fine underbrush. It all looks and feels so pristine.

We get back in the van, with the tentative plan to drive down another 30 miles West to the nearest campervan site. We look for a coffee shop or other food store to have a quick bite and rest. But we find none. Paola and I reason that in fact it looks like there is not much else to see here in Arthur Pass.

It's fun and liberating that we have no minute-by-minute plans, that every day we decide what to do next. We have no hotels booked. I made a tentative travel itinerary, but make sure everyone while I drive reviews it, looks at travel guides and the brochures we pick up along the way, and votes and advices on what to do next.

So here Paola and I make the quick executive decision to just drive back on route 73 towards Christchurch, but before getting to it turn right on route 77, and head towards Mount Cook, which will be our next big site to visit.

We know this is way too far, as it's already about 6pm, and from Arthur's Pass to MtCook there are an estimated 195 miles, or 4 hours, of driving. I had printed from the internet (www.holidayparks.co.nz) a few pertinent pages of the best campervan sites in South Island, which turned out to be extremely helpful. We only pick sites with electricity, facilities, and water; in short, all included. One campersite, number 25, Glentunnel Holiday Park, should be only about a two, two-and-a-half hour drive from Arthur Pass: doable. This will also allow us to get on our way much sooner, compared to our rough itinerary, and so hopefully drive much less tomorrow.

The various sources of information we had gathered said that some of these camper sites can book quickly and be full, so, even if we are not in high season, but at the end of summer and really beginning of fall, I call ahead. My cell phone works well, just 00 first, then 64 for New Zealand, then the number 3 for most places in South Island, before the actual telephone number. The nice lady on the phone tells us that there is space. When I inquire, she also says their reception closes at 9pm.

On the way, we stop for dinner at the only restaurant we find, in a very small town called Sheffield. It's more like a tavern. Only about three other tables are occupied, clearly by locals. We all have meat dishes. I have rack of lamb, calling it 'rock of lamb' as I see it written with chalk on the menu of the day. In one of the nearby tables, there are about eight girls, about 17 year old, celebrating a birthday. They are all pretty much blond and light eyed. They often throw glances at the two tall and handsome strangers sitting at our table.

Without rushing, as the speeding limit is 100 km an hour (about 55 miles an hour) throughout New Zealand, I get to the camper site at about 8:30pm, making perfect time. Of course, these official encounters are all mine, as Paola hates them. The lady, as all Kiwis I meet during the whole trip, is super-nice. She assigns us spot number 52, and gives me a map of the site so I can find it. Even if outside it's pitch dark, I do find it.

In darkness, with only some stars peeking through the clouds, I spot the electric pole where I plug the extension to power the campervan. I later venture out again to visit the toilet facilities, which look better than expected, and are only about 10 meters (30 feet) from our camper, behind tall trees. We get set for our first night in a campervan. I leave on the shirt, and wear pajama top and pants, as well as socks, to keep warm. We have certainly earned our rest. The night is a bit cold initially, then Paola puts the heater on.

Tuesday March 25

As usual, I'm the first to wake up. While it is initially dark when I first start waking, still forcing myself to sleep more and get adjusted to the new time zone (we are 18 hours ahead of Philadelphia), I continue to pick through the curtains until I finally see some light coming through.

I do not want to wake anyone up, so I do not get out of bed (space is very limited anyway), but just lean over and get the laptop. The early hours in the morning are always my favorite ones to write. While I'm a bit hungry, I enjoy the time to just follow my thoughts and memories, to relish the quietness, and to savor the slow rise in intensity of the light which is accompanying my first New Zealand sunrise.

Slowly, one after the other, Paola, then Pietro, then Andrea, as per tradition during the rest of this trip, wake up. Now that I can move without fear of waking them, I transfer to my favorite first activity of every morning, showering. With two fifty NZ cents in my hand, I go to the facilities building. I'm the only one there, even if it's already about 9am. The place is actually immaculate, as all these campersites throughout New Zealand will always be. Incredibly clean, spotless, white, even if frequently used.

As instructed by the signs, once in one of the shower booths, I go naked, and then put the money in the slot to start the water. Somehow, I think that I have put on 4 minutes worth. So I quickly shampoo and clean myself well everywhere, to get rid of the dirt accumulated after such a long trip. But the shower does not seem to want to stop. I later realize that each 50 cents gave me 4 minutes, so the warm steady stream lasts for 8 wonderful minutes. I'm a new man, all rejuvenated.

The rest of the family is now fully awake and in activity. Paola does not want to shower or go to bathroom facilities at all. She said I had promised she could always use the camper bathroom. Andrea and Pietro instead grab each 50 cents, and I show them the great public facilities. They also greatly enjoy the shower while I shave.

We have breakfast together. While Paola attempts to use the bathroom, we go around the campersite. Led by a campersite map, Andrea Pietro and I follow a path and find a river parallel to the hill in front of us. It's about 15 feet wide. The water is super clear. We walk for a bit upstream along the river, as Andrea finds a path. There is a sign warning about not jumping in the water, as the red algae are apparently poisonous. It is wonderful to have the three of us together on this small adventure in uncharted territory.

Once back driving, we decide not to turn towards Methven, where we could take a balloon ride, as it is definitely too rainy and overcast to do so. Continuing on route 72, we pass Mt Somers, Mayfield, and arrive in Geraldine. Pietro has been complaining of some pain in his head in addition to the continuing discomfort of the toothache, and has cold symptoms, so here we get some meds for his apparent cold at the local pharmacy. The lady inside tells us upon my asking that there are 2,500 people in Geraldine, about 3,000 with the surroundings. She says it like this is a big important town, which I have to admit so far it's accurate, compared to what we have seen along the road so far.

We have a wonderful lunch in Geraldine in a little New Zealand bistro - Verde' - with great food and atmosphere. Paola picked it, while we were walking around under the light rain. I have a lentil salad. We also have desserts, and coffee drinks, all delicious. The staff is friendly, very courteous. The clientele is upper-class looking, all white, while casually dressed. I try to go the bathroom, with meager results despite the clean facility.

Back on the campervan, we turn from route 72 to route 8. We drive in pouring rain for hours. We pass a town called Fairlie. During the ride I talk with Pietro and Andrea about their personal issues, school, love, dreams. They take turns in the navigator seat next to me, as Paola continues to organize the van. They are happy kids, as I know and now confirm. Andrea got 96 in his latest math test, and an A in English for his Manifesto on how all people should speak at least one foreign language. Pietro tells me about his looking forward to spending the summer on the beach in Tarquinia, Italy, with friends, and to playing basketball once he gets into high school at Germantown Friends School near Philadelphia in the fall, hoping to be a swing player between varsity and junior varsity.

We arrive at a beautiful site, Lake Tekapo. It's still cloudy, but not raining anymore. We stop at the Church of Good Shepherd as suggested by our travel guides. It is a tiny stone structure on a small lookout near the lake shore. Behind the altar, there is a huge window with a spectacular view of the lake. This is a lovely place, made a bit more mystical by the weather and the cold. I kneel down, and pray. We ask some people to take a picture of us with the lake view inside the church. Pietro is not feeling well, is tired, and gets back in the van. The three of us walk some more on the banks of the lake. The natural beauty is breathtaking.

Once we leave, less than a kilometer down the road, Andrea sees a sign for Mt John. I pull the van to the side of the road a bit abruptly, and we all democratically decide to turn. It's only 4pm, we have time, and I love the spontaneity of following what others propose. It turns out to be another great decision. The winding and steep road takes us up to the summit of the mountain, where the Mt John Observatory sits.

We park, and it's cold outside, and a bit windy. We spot the bathrooms, which we all visit, and the Earth and Sky Café up on top. We get hot chocolate and a wonderful moist chocolate brownie. I strike a conversation with the young and tall waitress, as I do everywhere, to get tips and stories from locals. She is actually from France, living here for the last four years, as she is going out with a Kiwi boyfriend.

I also inquire about the recommended observatory tours, during which on certain nights one can see the Southern Lights, but its too late to book, and the trips would leave anyway at 7:30 or 9pm, which is too late for our plans. We take in again the great view, which one can enjoy from stepping outside, but also from inside, as the café walls are all glass from floor to ceiling for at least 270 degrees around. Pietro spots the tiny Church of Good Shepherd on the shore of the lake down below.

We drive towards Mt Cook, passing another, even bigger lake, Lake Pukaki. It's overcast, as often here, so along our way we cannot discern any of the marvelous mountain peaks we are supposed to see according to our guides. But we can continue to learn about our next destination.

Regarding Mt Cook, called by Maoris 'Aoraki,' the Maori legend says that Aoraki was one of three sons of the sky father, Rakinui. Their canoe was caught on a reef and frozen, forming the South Island. In fact, Maoris call the South Island *Te Waka O Aoraki*, or Aoraki's canoe. The highest peak is Aoraki, frozen by the south wind, and turned into stone.

Interestingly, Aoraki was first climbed successfully by three New Zealanders in 1894, just after it was announced that an English and an Italian climber were about to attempt the ascent. National pride succeeded.

We do eventually arrive at the tiny Mt Cook village, where just about 70 people live in the winter, and at most 300 in the summer, as temporary workers get busy with tourism jobs. After a bit of driving around, Andrea points me in the right direction for the Hermitage Hotel, the best in town and apparently the highlight of this settlement.

The Hermitage is a luxury hotel, new given its rebuilding in 2005 after a fire. It's mostly glass and steel, a marvel. Its two communicating towers with their ten floors dominate the village below. Pietro's face is quite swollen, especially on the right side. He has not been feeling great, taking ibuprofen for facial discomfort for the last couple of days. I sense this is no allergy. He has no fever, and a normal heart rate.

Soon after we enter in the hotel, Paola approaches me saying that Pietro would love to stay here at the hotel overnight, and not in a campersite. I feel bad for him, and inquire about a room for us. The only one available is a superior suite at NZ$499, but I go for it, as a present to poor Pietro, who I hope will be better after a good night sleep in a regular bed.

I also ask about a doctor. The check-in staff tells me that the closest is in Twizel, about an hour back from where we came on route 80. They give us the telephone number for the Medical Center, 03 435 0777. I immediately call, putting a +64 for the country code, and omitting the '0' before the '3.' We can get an appointment for 3:40pm the next day, the earliest available.

After having populated our splendid room, with a floor-to-ceiling glass window looking straight at MtCook, we go to the Alpine Center, located in the same hotel and dedicated to Edmund Hillary and his ascent to Everest.

In the Cinema Planetarium, we watch two movies, one about Mt Cook, and the other about the unique story of New Zealand animals. Originally, only birds made it here to New Zealand, and lived with no other big animal around. In fact, as there were no mammals, many birds with time gave up flying, as there were no predators on the ground. The national bird, the Kiwi, is a perfect example of this strange evolution, with wings which are barely identifiable now, stronger legs, and a long beak able to poke the soil to eat seeds, berries and small insects.

Mt Cook National Park contains 72 named glaciers, and 22 mountains peaks. We learn about Aoraki/Mt Cook, which is the highest mountain in Oceania, at 3,754 meters, or 12,316 feet. Hillary trained as a young man here, before ascending Everest in 1953. There are National Park glaciers, boat tours, and many other options to enjoy this natural paradise. At the Activity Center, I book the activities for the next day: a scenic flight to Tasman Glacier with Andrea at 9am (Paola and Pietro decline), and an 11am glacier-lake boat tour for all us four.

As the movies end at 8:15pm, we move to the buffet dinner, previously booked. The food is good and abundant, but not five stars as one would expect. I have three different types of salmon, all delicious. After dinner, Pietro and Paola are tired and go to the room. I am not one to miss any opportunity, and propose to go to the 9pm show at the Planetarium. Andrea, interested, happily joins me.

The Planetarium show is awesome. The Kiwi live narrator does a wonderful job of describing the big bang and how galaxies and stars are organized. But his best feat is to explain to us the stars of the Southern sky here in New Zealand. Here it is, in brief summary. One should first find two aligned bright stars. These are the so called 'Pointers.' If one follows the line between these two stars, one can then easily identify the famous Southern Cross!!!

The Southern Cross is a rhomboid structure with four stars. Putting a line at a 90 degrees angle with the Southern Cross as coming from the Pointers, this will point to Orion. In between this line, one can see on each side two other galaxies!!! These are the Major and Minor

Magellanic Clouds. So not only we can see the hazy brightness of our Milky Way as a fuzzy horizontal cloud across our sky, but, for the first time in my life, I can see these other two galaxies.

Interestingly, Orion can also be seen in the Northern Hemisphere, but here in the Southern it is upside down, with the stars for the knees above the belt, and the stars for the shoulders below it. One can also easily see the stars making Orion's sword, which I had never seen before. Continuing with his excellent and clear explanation, the narrator tells us now to follow Orion's belt, which leads us to Sirius, another bright star. Of course, the best part of the show is to see Andrea so interested, mesmerized.

Following the Planetarium show, which ends at about 10pm, the narrator invites us for another hour of gazing at the stars outside, weather permitting. Andrea is more mature and socially correct than me, and decides that we should instead go to our room, so not to be too late. Paola was already not too happy about us leaving her and Pietro earlier.

Nonetheless, Andrea and I have to step outside to pick up our night staff from the campervan. The sky is incredible!! There is not one cloud, and one can see all the stars. In fact, the narrator had told us that it's easier to identify stars on the real sky than in the Planetarium. We can see now how he was absolutely correct. Andrea identifies quickly and easily the Pointers, Southern Cross, Orion, and the three galaxies. What a magic, unforgettable night.

Wednesday March 26

I get up at 6:30, and immediately step out of our hotel room, so not to wake anyone else up. I keep a long-sleeved polo shirt and my pajama pants. I write a bit about this trip in peace in a semi-deserted lobby, when outside is mostly still dark. As instructed, as soon as the elegant coffee shop opens at 8am, I get a cappuccino for Paola. There are often clouds obscuring Mt Cook's summit, but today the sky is mostly clear. Mt Cooks dominates the stunning view from the large windows of our magnificent hotel room, on the ninth floor.

All together we have a quick breakfast of cookies and milk in the hotel room. Then, as planned, Andrea and I go downstairs at 8:50am to get picked up for the plane ride to the glacier. A nice young Kiwi picks us up in a van. We drive about 5 minutes to the tiny airfield. Mike is a 60ish year old bear of a man who will fly us in the Skyplane to the park's glacier, with the hope of landing, if the weather is still clear, the winds low, and the snow packed enough, on Tasman's Glacier.

An almost-retirement age couple from Chicago will also take the flight with us. They are nice enough to allow Andrea to sit up front, next to Mike. I joke and say to not let Andrea drive too much, as he just got his permit. Mike says that then he'll do the takeoff, and let Andrea do the landing. He is a good sport. The plane has about eight seats, Mike and Andrea up front, the Chicago couple in the middle, and me in the last row, by myself.

Right on time at around 9:30am, Mike lifts the small mono-engine propeller plane from the runway pointing directly towards the tall mountains in front and above us. He tells us that the weather forecast is for high winds up there, and that we possibly could not be able to land, in which case we would get a refund. We are also told it might be bumpy up in the mountains. Despite a bit of fear in my heart, Mike seems reassuring, confident, and careful.

Thankfully, the forecast is dead wrong. We fly fairly smoothly for such a small plane. Mike veers close to the mountains on our right, and describes the sites, the different glaciers below, the Terminus Lake, the few icebergs, the mountains above, in particular Mt Cook slightly on our left. We quickly get to one of the highlights, Tasman's Glacier. This is the biggest glacier in New Zealand, at about 27 km (about 17 miles) in length. While the bottom 'tongue' of the glacier is covered with stones, up here the glacier appears as a glistening white smooth surface. I figure it's around here that any landing can be tried.

Mike goes up near the top on the glacier, and lowers the plane, warning us of possible bumps. He makes the plane just touch the snow for about 20 meters or so going downhill, and I wonder how in the hell he'll stop the plane going so fast on slick snow and on a downhill slope. But he pulls back and lets the plane detach away from the snow's surface. An aborted landing? What went wrong?

Mike with his microphone alerts us all is well. He gently turns the mono-engine around, and now points it uphill for the true final landing on the glacier. It is a quite smooth and safe. As we land, he explains that the first brief landing was a trial. We are the first flight of the day, there is fresh snow from the night before, and he wanted to make sure the snow below us was hard enough and not too soft and deep, so to allow a safe landing.

He lets us deboard, and get on the glacial snow. There is indeed a two-inch-deep layer of fresh snow, but below this, it feels quite packed. Mike is surprised that the temperature was not below zero overnight, as the snow is not ice as he had predicted. In fact, we have a clear sky above out heads, and we are surrounded by the magnificent spectacle of Mt Cook and its adjacent other peaks and glaciers. There is almost no wind, barely any breeze actually, and the sun is very bright up here. In short, it is pleasant, beautiful, not cold. And we are the only souls up here. I feel elated, blessed.

One gets a sense of wonder of how beautiful our world is. Mike tells us a bit more about the glacier. We can also walk around a bit, and enjoy the silence of the majestic place. Its purity. Our insignificance as human beings compared to the beauty and grandiosity all around us. For Andrea and I this will be an unforgettable experience. An undeletable memory.

After a smooth ride back, flying right next to the blue and white pointy glaciers on the side of Mt Cook, Mike drives us back himself to the Hermitage Hotel. He says he had guessed I was a physician by my demeanor. When asked, he admits he has been doing these flights up the glacier for over 19, almost 20 years, and, he reveals, "I'm a bit embarrassed to admit that." He is really a nice guy. He is concerned about Pietro, who I told him is due to see the doctor in Twizel at 3:40pm. Mike is from Twizel, and he's glad we are seeking professional help.

Andrea and I get back just in time to the Hermitage at MtCook Village. As planned, we walk in the Adventure Activities shop at 10:45am, to meet Pietro and Paola for the booked boat trip on Terminus Lake to see up close the lower edge of the Tasman Glacier. We are excited, elated for the great adventure just enjoyed and for the new one coming right up.

The four of us though are getting more worried about Pietro, whose right side of the face is very swollen. The edema is getting worse, even if his pain is mild to non-existent now. The diagnosis of tooth abscess seems even more obvious now. While waiting to be picked up again to go to the lake, I text our friend Bill to ask for his partner Carlos's cell number, as he is a dentist we trust in Philadelphia.

We get to the Terminus Lake area. From the parking lot, we walk about two miles to the lake shore, escorted by friendly young guides. The weather is gorgeous, sunny, mild, I'd say 'pure.' Our friend Bill texts me indirect advice from Carlos for Pietro to take penicillin, reassuring us that this should suffice. I'm a bit amazed there is reception for my cell this far from 'civilization.' Once on the shore, we don life jackets, and board boats accommodating about 12 people each. The guide in our boat is a friendly Brit who has been living in NZ for about 8 years, and loving it.

Basically, Terminus Lake is a very recent lake formed by the melting of the glacier. In fact it sits at the end of the Tasman Glacier. It began to be formed only about 25 years ago, and it is now over 7 km (4 miles) long! It is growing in length about a foot per week! On the other side of where we board, the head of the glacier is receding 300meters a year! One can see directly here how geology works.

While we take off from the simple dock, Carlos himself, our friend the dentist in Philadelphia, texts not to worry, and just to give penicillin to Pietro. It's amazing how we can communicate from a glacial lake in the middle of nowhere, near a town (Mt Cook village) of 70 people at the foot of huge mountains in New Zealand's South Island. I feel a bit out of contest sending messages on my iPhone from this natural paradise, but the cause is certainly an important one.

On the boat, we approach some of the icebergs on the lake. There are probably only about 10 of these today in the lake, of varying forms and shapes, about 3 to 8 feet high and 3 to 10 feet wide. From up close, one can appreciate, as the guide points them to us, the features. About 10% of an iceberg's mass is above water. The water reshapes constantly the glacier, especially at water edge level, where an indentation can be seen, making the iceberg 'skinny' here.

As this water erosion occurs, the glacier often turns on itself, as its mass has shifted. So often one can see these deep dents up on the iceberg, as the frame has rotated and part of the former base is now out of the water. The guide also points to the colors of the iceberg, often white, but also electric light blue, or greyish, depending on the organization of its crystals. Fascinating.

I feel bad, but the guide a couple of times tears off some pieces of the iceberg to make us appreciate up close its composition, purity, and crystals. I'm sitting up front and close to the edge of the boat, so I get first-hand view of them. There are an almost infinite number of these crystals coming off the glacier every week. The guide also tells us that these crystals were formed up in the mountain about 300 years ago, which is the time it takes snow from just being fallen, to become part of the glacier, and then over centuries come down slowly down the side of the mountain, until breaking off at the edge of the lake. So the bubbles inside the ice can be used by scientists to determine the quality and composition of air 300 years ago.

The friendly Brit takes us then to about less than half a mile from the edge of the glacier. The 'wall' formed by the glacier's mass as it arrives to the lake is impressive, even this far away. We cannot get closer as at times large masses of ice break off, and large waves are formed. A few years ago, one such wave arrived at the dock on the other side of the lake causing major damage up to 30 feet high.

We can clearly see that the bottom edge of the glacier is constantly being eroded by the water, and so the base where the ice sits is quickly disappearing. As the weight of the ice exceeds what is below it, a chunk breaks off and forms a new iceberg. Our guide says that he remembers times the lake was barely navigable given the hundreds and hundreds of icebergs on it.

I have studied the geophysics of glaciers many times: I finally understand now exactly how they really form, move, change, and eventually disappear. It is estimated Lake Terminus will soon extend another few miles south and join the huge Lake Pukaki. The ever warmer water will continue to quickly erode the quickly disappearing glacier.

On our way back on the boat, we are pointed to notice the sides of the lake. These have over-100-feet-tall eroded rock walls, clearly shaped by the old sides of the glacier. One's mind drifts to imagine the landscape here just a few hundred years ago. So much has changed. Similar events have happened almost everywhere else in the world, but this is the first place I've ever been where I can see and understand them with my own eyes.

Back by 1:30pm, we have a quick lunch at the Coffee Shop of the Hermitage Hotel. I again eat plenty, including a salmon and bacon pie, and a salmon and vegetable quiche, plus a big yogurt. Mt Cook has been a marvelous place to visit. We leave at 2:15pm to Twizel for the 3:40pm appointment with the doctor.

As I look and think about Pietro, I'm getting more worried. These are tense moments, when a parent wonders if coming so far, on the other side of the globe, was worthwhile, being so distant from any hospital. Paola asks me what could go wrong, and I tell her I'm worried he could get septic and need intensive care, and also I'm wondering if his eye will get more involved in the infection as well. I need to make her aware of what I'm thinking, as two heads as better than one in these anxious moments.

Twizel is small, and the sign saying 'Town Centre' is in a crossroads with few scattered one-story buildings around it, with a parking lot where we leave the campervan. This looks like a small village rather than a town. Our address – 37 Tasman Road - points to one of these small seemingly frail and wooden dwellings, in front of which the words 'Medical Centre' are written. In the US, this would look more like a small one-story rural café.

While we wait over an hour at the general practitioner office in Twizel, I wonder if we'll need to go back to Christchurch for a hospital, or even if we'll need to fly out of New Zealand in need of even more specialized oral surgical help, or intensive care. I'm not worried at all we'll miss most and probably the best part of our trip. I'm more worried anything bad may happen to Pietro, a huge joy of my life. I would give anything now to make him better. Anything.

At the Twizel Medical Centre, once we finally get to see the doctor, Annie Fyfe, we have a satisfying visit. She is nice, and gets the diagnosis right away. She can tell there is a large abscess, and shows us a diagram of the right maxilla, saying that Pietro's maxilla is full of pus. She is afraid a hole may need to be drilled by a surgeon in the roof of Pietro's mouth to drain the abscess. She is fearful the abscess is high enough to begin to affect Pietro's right eye, which in fact is already a bit swollen and cannot open as much as the left eye from the inflammation below.

She calls first an ENT in Christchurch, then an oral surgeon in Dunedin for phone consultations and lots of questions. I'm impressed how easily she gets them on the phone, and how helpful they are, with long conversations. She is clearly very worried. After getting all these phone consults, from kind and knowledgeable colleagues, she chooses the second recommendation.

She goes out for about five minutes, and returns as promised with 1.2grams of Augmentin in a 20cc syringe. She gets a bit frazzled when she understands I'm a doctor, and says I would probably do a better job than she would. She is a bit shy, cautious, but caring and compassionate. She is originally from Wanaka, and we get to know her a bit personally while she assists us so well.

She wonders at some point if any of our boys would become physicians. I tell Andrea and Pietro that her specialty is one of the most difficult, as she needs to be able to diagnose and treat any ailment. She shrugs her shoulders at the compliment, saying, "We are jakes of all trades, masters of none." She injects the yellow fluid in Pietro's arm vein without difficulty, flushing it with three 20cc-saline-syringe pushes.

She also gives us about 20 Augmentin tablets, each 625mg, for Pietro to take every eight hours, plenty to last until we get back to the US. Augmentin is amoxicillin clavulanate, a strong form of penicillin, an antibiotic well-known to me, and basically what I was hoping for. She tells us repeatedly to go to Alexandria, apparently close to Queenstown, to a dentist. If Pietro needs oral surgery, he would be referred to Dunedin, where the closest university hospital is located.

She has been outstanding. I'm delighted Pietro is finally on this penicillin-containing strong antibiotic, which should by itself, as Carlos our friend the dentist in the US had stated, be enough to quiet things down without further emergency interventions. I pay NZ$145 ($116), all included, which is money very well spent.

Paola and I discuss future plans and alternatives a lot during our drive south-west towards Queenstown. From Mt Cook to Queenstown there are 162 miles, or 3 hour and 5 minutes of driving, and we have the vast majority of this distance left from Twizel, which we leave a bit after 5:30pm, after an over-an-hour-long visit.

As we drive on route 8, through Omarama and then Landis Pass, we decide to make an appointment with a dentist in Queenstown, which looks like a big town anyway, and where at least we can start to see a dental expert. The plan is to call tomorrow Thursday early in the morning, and make that our first order of the day, before planning anything else. Pietro's health is securely at the top of our priorities. We drive on and pass through Tarras, Cromwell, and then turn into route 6.

We arrive in Queenstown at 8:30pm, and pull in a top 10 campersite, Creeksyde, very close to the center of town, in fact walking distance. We are given once again a site (#21) near the bathroom facilities, which is most convenient. After having parked and plugged in the electricity, we walk the ten minutes to the center of Queenstown. It's now dark outside.

Queenstown immediately impresses us. For the first time in New Zealand, we are strolling in a real town, with people walking around, activity in the streets, and modern shops. We get the feeling of a vibrant city. We have dinner, at the kids request, and against Paola's wish, at KFC, Kentucky Fried Kitchen. We devour over 30 pieces of fried chicken, while Paola has a salad.

We then walk a bit more around. The town is elegant, with lots of young people, mostly in their twenties. Once in the campervan, I worry again all night. I pray for Pietro's right face, still very swollen and unrecognizable, to get better. I can't wait to get another opinion, this time from an expert in the field. Double-checking is the minimum we can do for Pietro.

Thursday March 27

As we get up in the morning, I take the usual shower. Again the facilities in this campersite are super clean. Even Andrea and Pietro take a shower. We'll never poop in the campervan, none of us. As usual, we also have breakfast together in the RV, mostly with the cookies we had bought the first day in Geraldine, which will last, perfectly, just to the last day breakfast.

I wait until 9am to call what looks like the most centrally located and best dentist in Queenstown, John Molloy. He is the first listing when I google 'Queenstown dentist.' The receptionist gives me an appointment that morning for 11:15am, saying to come in by 11am for the paperwork. I'm very happy I can get this appointment so soon.

We then decide that we'll move out of the campersite, and look maybe for a reasonably priced hotel in Queenstown. The heater in the camper is in fact noisy, and I again do not sleep well in the very early morning, when it's coldest outside and the heating system makes the most clattering, really annoying sound. Moreover, condensation forms on the plastic ceiling above Pietro and Andrea, and so water drips over them during the night. We all vote for a better sleeping arrangement for the next night.

So I step out of the campersite by 9am, with my running shoes, and go to the nearest couple of hotels, which are even closer to the center of town. One is a boutique hotel that Paola has seen wishfully the night before. Unfortunately the only availability is a two-bedroom suite at NZ$599. Thanks, but no thanks. I go to the Motel close to it, where a nice girl says there are no availabilities there, but we could stay at a sister location, the Lomond Lodge, even closer to the town center. The cost is only NZ$245 for a two-bedroom apartment. This sounds a lot more reasonable.

The other order of business is where to park the campervan that night in Queenstown. While looking for the campersite, the night before Paola had spotted a large nearby outdoor carpark (as they are called here). After a couple of wrong turns, we find it. We plan to leave the car there until 6pm, paying happily just NZ$2.50 at the automatic booth. In the center of Queenstown, Paola and I waste a few minutes talking to the manager at the local Sofitel, which has outrageous prices.

We then walk together to nearby Lomond Lodge. Lauren, the nice receptionist, says they do not have rooms at the Lodge, but they have instead available a nice two-bedroom apartment in the town center, on 44 Beach Street. Without even seeing it or knowing exactly where it is, we book it for the NZ$245. We are relived we have a place to stay. We tell Lauren we'll be back by about 6pm to pick up the keys, when our paid meter expires for our campervan parking.

We inquire to Lauren where we should park the campervan overnight, but she is not sure. By asking other people around town, we discover that parking after 6pm until 8am the next morning in normal city streets as in public parking lots in Queenstown is free. I'll just get up before then as I naturally do, and come and put more coins in the meter.

We are ready now to go to the dentist. We refrain from making any plans after. We do know that Queenstown is adrenaline central, full of great activities such as whitewater rafting, water skiing and rafting on the lake, parasailing, hiking, a Gondola ride to top of Bob's Peak, a cruise across Lake Wakatipu, 4WD safaris, scenic flights, paragliding, and many others. My real wish is to take the skyline gondola to the top of mountain (Bob's Peak), and then mountain bike down, as the travel guides suggest to do.

The dentist office is right in the center of town. The reception area is large, elegant, white, with two large floor-to-ceiling windows looking over the main square and the bay. I am reassured we are in a reputable place, even better than I could guess from their prominent website, www.queenstowndentist.co.nz. The receptionist is a cute and serious young blond girl. I soon find out she serves as nurse, too. I fill out the brief health questionnaire and hand it to the nurse, together with a type-written note about Pietro's history and therapy so far from the wonderful and caring doctor in Twizel.

Right on time, around 11:15am, John Molloy the dentist comes out, smiles, and calls for Pietro. He looks like the picture in the website. Andrea prefers to stay in the waiting room, Paola and I accompany

Pietro inside. It takes about two minutes for the dentist to get the diagnosis and plan his next move. Soon he says, as we are describing symptoms and history to him, and he is reviewing the document from Twizel, "I like these things." He takes a few x-rays. He shows them to Paola and me, pointing to the inflammation and infection just above Pietro's right main incisor.

He says that some of this tooth died slowly after Pietro broke it six months ago while hitting himself with a racket, accidentally. The necrotic pulp lured in bacteria, which are now the cause of the abscess and facial swelling. The antibiotics are a great first step. He also now wants to drill a small hole in this tooth, get to the bottom of it, and, I understand, try to drain the pus.

Paola decides to step out, and I stay behind, with the dentist's permission, to keep Pietro company. Slowly, methodically, carefully, and using tiny instruments and microscopic glasses, John Molloy drills a tiny hole in the back of Pietro's sick incisor. He soon pulls out the mushy pulp, which is mostly black from necrosis. He keeps on taking x-rays, until he confirms he is at the end of this very long tooth, which almost exceeds the length of his instruments. "A long tooth in a long person," he states. Pietro is 14, but he's already over 6'4" tall.

The dentist cannot pull out any pus, though. He says the roof of the tooth must be clogged by inflammatory cells. But he seems happy, saying, "We have taken away the cause of the abscess." In his experience, just doing what he just did would cure the problem, even without antibiotics. He closes the small hole with calcium hydroxide, which he says will further inhibit bacterial growth. During the almost-one-hour-long procedure, Pietro requires almost no anesthesia, and never flinches. He is tough, mature, and makes me proud.

John Molloy looks confident, and happy about his successful intervention. I'm a bit bummed that he did all that but did not get any pus out. We let Paola back in. I insist a bit asking what are we to do if Pietro gets worse. Call him back? Call an oral surgeon? Go to the hospital? The dentist is smiling, reassuringly, saying he sees at least five or six of these a year, and they always improve after his surgical intervention. Finally, he states, "For sure you call me back if he does not improve. But he will."

The bill from the nurse/receptionist is NZ$540. Dentists are expensive everywhere. I'm at my happiest though. Pietro has gotten now both medical and surgical therapy, and I'm reassured that we have him plugged in with seemingly competent clinicians. I have a big smile on my face, and I contaminate Paola, Andrea, and in particular Pietro, who has been wonderful throughout.

We can now plan our fun day in Queenstown. We walk up to the Gondola ride. Nearby, Paola Andrea and Pietro inquire about a visit to the Kiwi Park. They can get a combined ticket, first going up with the Gondola for a beautiful view of Queenstown and lunch on top of Bob's Peak, and then their plan is to come back to the Kiwi Park to admire the local birds. The show is at 3pm, and they do not want to miss it. It's about 12:30pm now.

I do want to take a mountain bike up Bob's Peak by Gondola and come biking down. At the nearby shop, I rent one, put on the helmet, protection for knees and elbows, and bike back up to the Gondola entrance. Andrea Pietro and Paola are clearly concerned I'm going to hurt myself, and not too happy I'm splitting from them. The compromise is that I'll get to bike ride only until 2pm, when we'll meet again at the bottom of the Gondola, in front of the Kiwi Park entrance. The kids want to do everything together as a family, and this will minimize our time apart.

So just from 12:30pm until 2pm, I get in two incredible bicycle rides down. On the first ride up, I meet Daniel, a 20-something Asian American from Silicon Valley. He says he fell at least five times on his first ride down, then he quit for a couple of hours while recuperating from the pain. He admits he used his front brakes, which he now understands he should not have. I confirm in my head to never use them, and to keep my right hand securely on the rear brake.

The thrill of adrenaline biking down Bob's Peak is one of the best I've ever felt in my life. The grading of the trails is similar to that of sky slopes: green, blue, and black, in increasing order of difficulty. I commit to just do the green ones. As later Andrea will point out, every other person biking down is in top shape and at least 20 years younger than me.

The path is treacherous, full of deep holes, jumps, very acute turns. If one were to get out of the two-to-three-feet-wide path, on the one side there is the mountain rock, and on the other a precipice. You not only would get hurt, I think you would not make it alive if you missed a turn and went straight down the mountain.

As I go down, I'm completely concentrated. Occasionally, I do gain a lot of speed even if I do not want to, given how steep certain parts of this green course are. At times, as I hurdle a bump, the bike quickly rises to my chin, and then, immediately after, falls out from under me. I ride mostly with my butt high away from the low seat, to avoid my private parts being crashed by the bumps. It's quite a work out.

I make it down in about 15-20 minutes without a fall. I'm sweating profusely, but elated. I have never stopped, coming down straight while most other riders take numerous stops down the course. I directly pull into the Gondola area to go up again. The only slightly unpleasant feeling is the stiffness in my right wrist, from the continuous breaking.

I get in a second, thrilling run. I take the same path, but choose at times the more difficult option down the path when two choices arise. After one huge bump, upon the steep descent the bike recoils against me as it lands on the ground, as I regain control. While I zip down, I find myself singing, at times swearing, fighting against the obstacles, like in a match between me and the treacherous track. I win, again, never falling or even putting a foot down the ground.

By 2:05pm, I've returned the bike, helmet and gear, and am in front of the Kiwi Park. But there is no sign of my three loved family members. I inquire to the reception girl, but she just arrived, and may have missed them. I go down to the official entrance, about 100 yards below a steep staircase and incline.

The three girls at the official park entrance have not seen a tall and thin brunette with two tall young boys. So I go back up, again, but still no sign of them. I look at the clock on my iPhone, it's still only 2:10pm. They must be running late. I leisurely now go back down again, to the store at the entrance of the Kiwi Park, and buy myself a protein bar, a chocolate bar, and a juice.

I take them up to where I was to meet Paola Andrea and Pietro, seat down on the bench, and finish sweating, while eating and drinking my light, well-earned lunch. About 10 minutes later, while I'm almost done eating, they appear, to my delight.

The Kiwi Park reveals itself to be an interesting place, and another good choice. The kids decide to visit first the Kiwi house. Inside it's very dark, with a faint red light shining just enough not to be pitch dark. Kiwis, interesting, are nocturnal animals. These birds, of Australian origin as most of the fauna here, were originally predated on by a huge eagle. To avoid it, they only came out at night. And, since there were no mammals or other predators on the ground, they stopped flying, and choose to get more comfortably their food from the ground. Flying is a very energy-expensive activity.

The huge eagle used to feed also on the moa, the prehistoric New Zealand large ostrich. But the moas were hunted to extinction by the Maori as these first humans settled in New Zealand about a thousand years ago. Consequently, the huge eagle, once it lost one of its primary food sources in the moa, also went extinct. The Kiwi birds, though, were by now used to only come out at night, and the extinction of their predators did not change their habits.

We visit the whole park, discovering plenty of rare birds that can only be found in this part of the world. Many are near extinction, and New Zealand is doing its best to revamp them. For example, we see a species of ducks with only 70 remaining birds of this type in the world. A different bird in the park is said by our audio guide to have only 25 remaining members of its species.

Probably the best part of our visit to Kiwi Park is the excellent show. A beautiful young brunette, with dark bleu eyes, a wide smile, plenty of passion, and the look of an explorer, together with a girl colleague, entertain us for over an hour. The theatre is outside, under a net, placed not to prevent the show birds from flying away, but to protect them from a free falcon which has disrupted some shows in the past.

The two young female rangers fly extraordinary types of parrots and geese right above our ears. They show us an opossum, of which there are way too many in New Zealand, even if it is not a local animal. The guide states that introducing mammals such as opossums, stoats, rats and others in New Zealand was perhaps one of the worst mistakes ever made here. In fact, she begs us to buy anything made with opossum fur. And, if we ever see an opossum on the road while driving, she urged us to squash it! There were over 80 million opossums in New Zealand until recently, and there are still 40 million, who are continuing to eliminate rare species not used to these relatively new predators.

After the Kiwi Park, at around 4:35pm, we head downtown for a stroll. Andrea is interested in visiting the Gardens along the bay, from his reading in the travel guide books. Paola and Pietro approve, and I go along. As we approach the pier, I see the signs for Jet Boat riding. This particular firm, KJet, goes down two rivers, one of them being the famous Shotover River.

I inquire when the next ride is, and the young blond fellow says it is in about 15 minutes, at 5pm, as the last ride of the day. While we walk to the Gardens, I announce I'm doing the jet boat ride. Andrea accepts to join me. Paola is mad I once again leave the main party, while Pietro happily decides to remain with her and quietly continue their stroll.

We put on long black plastic long-coat-like protectors to minimize getting wet, and life jackets. Andrea and I sit on the second row, just behind the crazy young driver. For an hour, we enjoy the thrill of jet boating, including frequent 360 degree spins. We get drenched several times. Andrea enjoys it, for the adrenaline rushes, and so do I, especially for seeing him happy. The river is pristine, and the jet is ecofriendly, being powered by a jet of water capable of 900 horse power.

As we deboard, I have to take my T-shirt off as it is all wet and I'm freezing. Andrea laughs at my boldness, as I do it in front of others. I put on back just my black fleece, which is plenty warm and still mostly dry. Soon after, on time at 6pm, Pietro and Paola stroll by, as planned. They had a good walk, and we had a good thrill. Everyone is happy.

After 6pm, we gather our belongings for the night from the camper, and head to pick up the keys of our apartment at Lomond

Lodge, as per plan with Lauren. We are only a few minutes late compared to our tentative meeting time of 6pm. We have to wait a few minutes as she helps check in two other groups, and then she happily walks us down to the center of town, where our apartment is, on Beach Street.

To our delight, we realize we must have gotten the best apartment in town! Inside, it's new, elegant, with huge rooms, all the amenities, a beautiful living room with access to a large balcony via the usual huge floor-to-ceiling bay windows. The terrace looks over the main square of Queenstown, the activity below, the bay on the lake, and the Remarkables mountains all around us. Wow!

After 7:30pm, we head out in search of a place to eat. Paola has proposed three choices from her reading all kinds of material. A French place, a fish place, and a local fare place. We stroll down the main pier and look at the menus of all the five or six restaurants in the main square and along the water. Paola cannot settle on any of them. The last one, though, gets us all exited, and we agree on it. It's the local food place Paola had on her list of three favorites, and looks wonderful.

The restaurant is called Public. The handsome Swedish waiter seats us, to our request, outside, and provides us with plenty of blankets. It's not that cold outside initially, but eventually I'll have three of them around me, as the temperature does come down a bit. The view is magnificent. They only sell food made within about 95 km (58 miles) of the restaurant. Kiwis in general try to eat what they make. I deeply admire them.

The food at Public is delicious. I have a huge salmon. Paola Andrea and Pietro each have large, delicious servings. They never serve bread here in New Zealand, as they produce little wheat. The dessert, in particular the Pavlova, made of meringue, vanilla ice cream, and kiwi fruit, is to die for. The waiter is impressed we cleaned up all the huge amount of food we ordered.

We have wonderful, lively, mature dinner conversation. Among other things, we confirm our plans for the next two days, our last full days in New Zealand. Tomorrow we'll try to get to Milford Sound, our last and fourth '1,000 places to see before you die' site. It may be tough to do it all in one day, but we'll try. We also decide to go on Saturday to Doubtful Sounds. So Friday night we'll get to Te Anau, on our way back from Milford Sound, and from there I'll be easy to get to lake Manapouri and Doubtful Sound. My hopes to get back for a full day in Queenstown to do a canyoning trip, as advised by my colleague Bud, vanish, as I definitively want to stay together with Andrea Pietro and Paola.

Friday March 28

As I get out of my morning shower, Pietro notices a red fresh bruise in my upper right abdomen, just below my rib cage. I was not aware of it. I remember and tell them that the day before, during my second mountain bike run down the mountain, I went over a huge bump and on the way down, loosing for a millisecond control of the handle bar, it hit my upper abdomen. I had not realized it could cause such a mark. But this has been the usual for me all my life, getting injured and not even noticing it.

As usual, I go and buy fresh donuts and croissants at the local bakery nearby, and we have breakfast together, in our beautiful apartment. Having the campervan makes moving from site to site extremely easy, as we only take night clothes and a change for the next day when we have hotel or apartment accommodations.

We vacate the apartment, sadly, after taking some pictures on the terrace. We then drive to Te Anau, about a two and a half hour beautiful easy drive south. I take route 6A (again a two-lane, two-way road, as all roads here in NZ) out of Queenstown, and then route 6 south. We travel alongside the shores of Lake Wakatipu on our right, with the fantastic view of the Remarkables mountain range on our left. Once again there is not much along the way even in terms of houses. We turn right at Five Rivers, and then right again at Mossburn to enter route 94 towards Te Anau.

We stop in Te Anau for lunch, at the first café we spot, as clearly there is not much civilization in the other half of the trip to Milford Sound. I have an eggs and bacon and toast plate, as does Pietro. We buy some huge local chocolate bars. We also enquire about the boat cruises for Milford Sound. The last ones are at 3:15pm and 3:45pm. It's already almost 1pm, we have more than 110 km of one lane, treacherous driving to go, so we need to get going!

After Te Anau the town, we continue on 94 along Te Anau the lake, on our left. The nature is just outstanding, the colors are vivid, pristine. The lake is light blue and brilliant. We enter Fiordland National Park, one of the '1,000 places to see before you die,' and New Zealand biggest National Park. Fiordland National Park is indeed huge, over 3 million acres. Rudjard Kipling said that Milford Sound was the Eighth Wonder of the World. In 1984, it was designated a World Heritage Area.

The drive to Milford Sound is a long winding road. We travel through beech forests, glaciated valleys, and a world as pure and wild as you can imagine it. The girl at the coffee house in Te Anau had given us brochures that highlighted about fourteen stops along the way. She said that two of them are a must. I make good time in the first part of this leg, so we have some spare time to stop at a few of these sites.

The first one is Mirrow Lakes. We find it at kilometer 58 after Te Anau, on the left side of the road. About six cars are parked alongside the road, one of the first signs of civilization we have seen after leaving Te Anau. Andrea Pietro and I ran out of the car to see it, Paola has her usual royal pace − she does not like to run. In front of us, huge mountains. Below us, who are now on a wooden bridge alongside the water, we see what looks like more of a river than a lake. It is a gorgeous sunny and clear day. It must be 60 degrees here in the sun. Andrea notices how one can see the mountain reflection in the water, perfectly. The water is still, clear as it can be.

Andrea also spots a sign, in the water. Upside down it says 'Mirrow Lakes,' and you can only read it looking at its perfectly clear reflection in the water. In fact, it's really a 'trompe l'oeil' ('something that fakes the eye, meaning some kind of optical illusion, from the French), as you notice and read first the reflection saying 'Mirrow Lakes,' and then you realize, after a few seconds, it's a mirror image of the upside down sign.

At kilometer 90 or so, we spot a sign for the Hollyford Valley Lookout. This offers a spectacular roadside view. The valley below is a jungle of greens, mostly dark and intense, with the weather now much cooler and completely cloudy. Above we can admire a huge mountain range, caressed by white clouds. All four of us are raptured by this gorgeous and majestic site. We take lots of pictures, aware that it's going to be hard to capture the power of this experience.

Soon after, we stop at the first light after 100 kilometers, as it's red, just before a long tunnel. This is called Homer Tunnel, we are at kilometer 101. We hesitate a moment if to stop here and enjoy the view, similar to the one we just saw at Hollyford Valley, but the light, which the guide says can stay red at times for 15 minutes, turns green, and we decide to go through.

The gradient down in the tunnel is 1 in 10, very steep; it feels like going to the center of the earth. The tunnel road is gravel, the sides are live wet dark rock, the tunnel is barely lighted, obscurity is all around us. The tunnel is 1219 meters long, unlined. The guide states that Homer Tunnel is a marvel of engineering which took 20 years to build, and was opened in 1954.

The last stop we make before arriving at Milford Sound is called the Chasm, at kilometer 109. In its parking lot, as we get out the car, we see at four or five feet in front of us, right next to the campervan, a Kea. We take several photo of this beautiful bird, unique to New Zealand. Its feathers are green externally, but orangy-red under its wings.

Then we take the twenty minute walk along this impressive 20-meter-deep crevasse, formed by the rushing waters of the Cheddau River. The loop forest walk lets us discover waterfalls everywhere, sculptured rock formations, magnificent trees and vegetation.

Paola Andrea and Pietro take lots of pictures. I begin to feel the light stings of the many sand flies of this forest. But they are not bad, only fastidious enough to remind me to put on long pants and long sleeves once I'm back on the campervan.

We arrive at 3pm at Milford Sound, and I immediately book the 3:45pm boat cruise, the last one of the day, just in time. The company is Fiordland Expeditions, and the boat is not one of the largest among the six or seven parked in the pristine waters of Deep Cove. The cruise is scheduled to last about two hours, and, when lucky, the passengers are supposed to catch sight of dolphins, fur seals, and gulls.

We spray some insect repellent while waiting inside, but mostly spend time on the dock admiring the huge mountains around the bay. Mitre Peak, the most famous of these mountains, is in front of us, dominating the view.

As soon as we sit down in the front of our boat, I start to converse with a New Zealand couple, Andrew and Catherine. They are from

Auckland, and super-friendly. We'll talk for much of the cruise. They have travelled the world together for two year straight a few years back, and have been to Philadelphia, Rome, and lots of other places we know well. They even traveled through Pescara. Andrea and Pietro are impressed.

Milford Sound is 9.3 miles long. Its sides are up to 4,000 feet high mountains, granite cliffs which come almost perpendicular into the icy Antarctic waters. Mitre Peak is the centerpiece, a 5,560-foot pinnacle whose peak if visible only occasionally through the clouds. It is one of the most photographed sites in New Zealand.

The Maori called New Zealand the Land of the Long White Clouds. Here in Milford Sound one finally realizes that indeed those who first visited these islands from the east (where most first explorers arrived from) must have found these west coast lands constantly covered by long white clouds.

The trip is unforgettable. This natural and uncontaminated land is like nothing I've ever seen in the world before. Here it does feel like everything is 100% pure. The Kiwis are right; in their islands nature is indeed special, unique.

The weather is how one would imagine it from studying the travel guides and looking at pictures. The temperature is at least 10 degree colder than inland, with a constant breeze, a certainly wetness in the air, overcast skies. It feels like we are leaving under a blanket of wet cotton.

In Milford Sound, it can rain up to seven meters (23 feet) of water a year. This is one of the rainiest parts of the world. There is so much rainfall here that the sea is topped by a 20-foot deep layer of fresh water! Our boat is gently cruising through this pristine ocean carved between mountains.

I spend most of the two hours on the top of our boat, despite the wind, cold, and dampness. I want to feel on my skin this Southern Hemisphere heaven, I want to meditate regarding all my blessing in life while immersed in this immaculate landscape. I want to take it all in.

The mountains around us are majestic. They come down sharply in the water at 70 to 80 degree angles. The primeval walls of rock are covered by trees. It's amazing how these trees can grow and stay attached on pure rock. They are of an intense dark green.

Occasionally, the wall of green is interrupted. The guide on the boat explains to us that once in a while there are tree avalanches, as they call them here. These occur when a tree outgrows its superficial roots, and falls down. This event makes the trees below also detach from the rock, so that a whole strip of mountain is bare of trees. The result is that a vertical patch of white rock is visible on the side of the mountain.

One of the other memorable sites is that of dolphins. Suddenly the windy silence is interrupted by the voice of the guide, which tells us to look in the front right side of the boat for a pod of dolphins. For the next 15 minutes or so, we have the most beautiful sighting of dolphins I've ever seen.

These Tasman Sea dolphins are each about 300 kilos, very large as to be able to survive in these cold waters. They swim right next to us, playing with our boat. They are of different shades of silver, and often come out of the water completely, doing their joyous flips.

They swim in large groups, which usually comprise twelve dolphins, and there are at least two pods following us, one very very close – I almost feel dangerously so - to the front of the boat, while the other is swimming and flipping right along the right side of our boat, which is now barely moving to let us enjoy the wonderful sight. Even the Maori guide says these are seen less than once per month, and is exited.

In the wonderful quieter moments of the cruise, Andrew, our new Kiwi friend from Auckland, tells us a lot of Maori legends. Maori are believed to have discovered Milford Sound more than 1,000 years ago, returning seasonally to the fjord, to collect the much prized *pounamu* (greenstone).

These treks from the east used traditional pathways across passes such as MacKinnon Pass on the Milford Track. The Maori named the sound *Piopiotahi* after the thrush-like piopio bird, which is now extinct.
The name Piopiotahi, means 'a single piopio,' harking back to the legend of Maui trying to win immortality for mankind - when Maui died in the attempt, a piopio was said to have flown here in mourning.

According to Maori Legend, Piopiotahi was carved out by *Tu-te-raki-whanoa*, an *atua* (godly figure) who was given the task of shaping the Fiordland coast. Chanting a powerful *karakia* (prayer), he hacked at the towering rock walls with his *toki* (adze) called *Te Hamo*. In 1912 John Grono was the first European settler to land in the sound. He named Milford Sound after Milford Haven in Wales.

As we cruise around, there are innumerable waterfalls visible on the sides of the mountains. At any point, one can often see multiple ones, some very thin, some bigger, some coming from very high in the mountains, some at times disappearing for parts of their paths behind the rock or among the trees.

We get very close to one of them, on the south side of Milford Sound. The roar of the water jumping down over the rock and diving sharply in the fjord gets louder. I begin to have to strain my neck looking up at the long cascade of pure transparent water.

The guide announces over the loud speakers that, if we want, we can go to the front of the ship, outside, for a 'Glacial facial.' Of course, I'm already in the front of our vessel. As we approach the side of the mountain, I begin to feel the spray of water hitting my face. Only a twenty-something hippy German girl is standing near me, as we drive slowly right under the waterfall.

The experience is sublime. As we move in, the sprinkle transforms in a hose of pure liquid, now drenching us. I'm well covered, with hat, impermeable North Face jacket, and jeans. I feel like in paradise. What fun! The water comes from glaciers up in the mountains, and the moniker 'glacial facial' is cute and appropriate. I would do one of these every day if I could. Better than a shower at home, which I still love.

Looking at each other dampen faces covered with beads of waterfall is fun. Taking the hat and jacket off inside the boat later is all I need to do to dry out. The whole trip to Milford Sound goes smoothly and perfectly, as almost everything else in this trip.

Soon on our way back, we see hitchhikers on the road. We had spotted a handful of others so far during our stay in New Zealand. Surprisingly, especially to myself, I stop the campervan to let on two young hikers, a young boy and a young girl. He has a beard, both are dressed casually. They are French. They sit in the back with our boys, and tell us their marvelous story. His English is decent, and I speak some French. They just need a short ride to a few miles down the road to a curve on the road where apparently other fellow hikers are waiting, to camp overnight. The boy and girl were each separately going to travel in New Zealand, met on the plane from Paris, and then decided to hike together! We leave them in what seems like the middle of nowhere, as dark clouds menace rain. A couple of young lads are indeed waiting for them on the rocky ground on the side of the street.

We arrive at our destination when it's now dark outside and past 8pm. We stop by many hotels and motels in Te Anau, but they are all booked. We eventually unanimously decide to stay at the local top 10 campervan site. The lady at the counter desk is super-nice, as all people in New Zealand, locals or newly acquired locals.

As I tell her our plan for the next day, she is very helpful and reserves for us the trip from Manapouri to Doubtful Sound. She books us the Wilderness Cruise with Real Journeys, one of the two major tourist agencies here in the South Island, which I had already studied as one if not the best. She also tells me to get some food before we board, as "it's cheaper and better."

We venture out of the campersite, under a sea of stars in the otherwise dark night, in search of a restaurant. It's almost 9pm, and the place is very quiet. While we look for alternatives, most are already closed, and so we settle on the one the lady at the campersite counter had advised us, the Redcliff Café, on 12 Mokonui Street, only about a short walk from our camper. I have the special fish of the evening. We do not eat much, only one order each, as we are just a bit too tired.

Saturday March 29

I get up once again to the rhythmic noise of the heating system in the campervan. Incessant. Impossible to sleep further, even if I try. I write a bit more, but this morning everyone has to get up a little early to drive to Manapouri and then eventually to Doubtful Sound. We have a very full day in front of us, and we are unclear regarding exactly what it is going to bring. We heard vaguely that we have a boat tour, that then we'll take a bus, then another boat to reach the coast and the Tasman Sea, and then back to base again through these three legs of the trip.

From Te Anau, we have a short twenty-minute ride to Manapouri, the city on the big homonymous lake. We get there around 9:45 am or so, and park in the tiny harbor. "We have forgotten to get food!" We decide that Paola and Pietro go and find the right boat and get in line, while Andrea and I run back towards the small shop with the sign 'Food' we had seen about half a kilometer from the gravel and grass parking lot.

What a run! It is probably unnecessary, as we get back in plenty time, but invigorating. The food is not great, as this is really a little country store with some simple meat sandwiches. I get way too much water and too many snacks for everyone. You never know.

Lake Manapouri, according to Maori legend, was formed from the tears of two sisters, *Motorau* and *Korowae*, daughters of an old chief in the region. The name Manapouri means something like 'Sorrowing Heart.' Indeed the weather is cloudy, almost misty, somewhat dark. It puts one in a pensive mood.

We board the Real Journeys vessel, which is about 40 yards long, not old, and in good shape. I take a seat on top and up front, to enjoy the astonishing view, while Paola Andrea and Pietro find a boot with table in the main cabin, in closed and warmer quarters.

The trip on Lake Manapouri is soulful, smooth, reflective. Like in Milford Sound, the nature is majestic, with tall rocky mountains covered by tall trees which cling to earth and give it life. I soak for a while the fresh air in the front of our boat, but soon it just feels a bit too cold and breezy. The wind moves the few brave tourists on top of the boat around, and a couple of them almost fall down from the power of the airstream.

The live loud speaker describes how restorative projects have freed some of these outer peninsulas and islands of stouts, rabbits, deer, and possums, mammals which are not local species, and whose introduction to these terrains has caused much damage to native fauna.

These mammals imported by the British colonizers caused the extinction of many of the native bird species. Birds flew here millennia ago, and since there were no predatory land mammals, over hundreds of thousands of yeas some of these birds had given up flying, which was no longer needed given they did not have to fly away from mammals. These lands have now been repopulated with indigenous endangered birds.

An alternative theory states that in the original Pangea, the primordial landmass on Earth, Zealandia separated from Australia and this allowed the development of a completely different set of species, unique to New Zealand.

After over one hour to traverse the splendid Lake Manapouri, we arrive at its western end, where we debark. We spend about fifteen minutes in a nice in-between station, where all facts about Doubtful Sound are narrated in short films and colorful posters. The guides encourage us to go to the bathroom, as they'll be no bathrooms for the next forty-five minutes or more. When we eventually board the buses, our group divides in two, a bus of mostly Chinese tourists, with Chinese-speaking guides, and another of mostly white tourists, with local New Zealand English-speaking guides.

The buses head to visit Manapouri Power Plant. This is the largest hydro power station in New Zealand, and one of the most efficient in the world. It uses the difference in water levels from the west arm of Manapouri Lake to Deep Cove in Doubtful Sound. Moreover, annual rain fall is one meter in Lake Manapouri, and eight meters in Deep Cove.

The initial 1960's plans were to elevate Lake Manapouri another 30 meters, but New Zealanders opposed it. It is said this was the birth of New Zealand's environmental consciousness. In fact, in 1996, a minimum flow of water was restored to the lower Waiau River to help reestablish the original environment.

The power plant is excavated in a cavern which goes 200 meters below the surface of Lake Manapouri. The first tunnels, eventually 10 km long and 10 meters wide, were initially built by 'drill and blast.' This meant often setting dynamite blasts, which had to be done in complete darkness to avoid explosions. The work took 1,800 workers eight years to complete in extremely hard conditions. Sixteen people died. The names of those killed are commemorated in a plaque. I stop in front of it, meditating about their lost lives. The plant was completed in 1972.

To generate power at higher levels and more efficiently, in 1993 a second tunnel was built, to allow water to flow away much more quickly. Technology had improved, and this second tailrace was built with a mammoth 25-meters-long tunnel-boring machine. At full power, now the plant has 500 cubic meter of water per second going through the station.

The plant has many floors, some above and some below sea levels. Interesting, now the power plant has usually only two people in it. One is a tourist guide, who is talking to us, and one is a guard. It is completely operated remotely, from far-off Christchurch, South Island's biggest city. One can only get to Manapouri power station by boat. 100% of the energy produced at this power plant is from renewable sources.

We leave the power station again by bus, and from the western end of Lake Manapouri we drive now towards Deep Cove, the eastern end of Doubtful Sound, where we'll again board a boat to visit our major destination for the day, Doubtful Sound. Ernest Wilmot discovered the pass that bears his name in 1897 and that lets us get through. The Wilmot Pass now allows us to take a bus, instead of having to walk through more difficult terrain.

The bus ride is beautiful in itself. Nature is disturbed only by our narrow gravel trail. On our initial ride up the mountains, on the east side, trees and brush are magnificent, but one would not call it a jungle. As we top the mountain and begin to come down the west side, the landscape changes to one that is much more wet, lush, tropical.

The trees here are a darker green, completely covered in moss, and very close to each other. The guide points out that, while on our way up one could have walked, with some difficulty, among the flora visible on the side of the road, here the jungle is dense and seemingly impenetrable. It's where some of the Lord of the Ring movies have been filmed. There are over 300 inches of rain a year in this area.

Once in Deep Cove in Doubtful Sound, we board a modern catamaran, the Patea Explorer. Doubtful Sound is much bigger than the still impressive Milford Sound. Here too tall mountains dive steeply into the deep blue waters, and continue to dive in even deeper, with the lowest point in the sound at 435 meters below sea level. Waterfalls, once again, come pouring down the deeply green mountainsides.

Glaciers – a word beautifully pronounced with a Kiwi accent - retreated from these grounds about 16,000 years ago, shaping the landscape. The rocks are made of lots of different, often precious and rare, minerals. The rock is very hard, 7.4 out of 10 on the hardness scale, according to our guide. I did not even know there is a scale to measure how hard a rock is.

These are new mountains, which have very little erosion. Many are shaped as when the glaciers were here. Maori legend has it that the demi-god *Tuterakiwhanoa* carved the present-day Fiordland landscape using his *ko* to dig out the steep-sided valleys and mountains.

The truth is that tectonic plates collide against each right here in Kiwi land. New Zealand is currently astride the convergent boundary between the Pacific and Australian Plates. Through most of the South Island, the plates slide past each other, with slight obduction of the Pacific Plate over the Australian Plate, forming the Alpine Fault and Southern Alps. From Fiordland south, the Australian Plate subducts under the Pacific Plate. It is fascinating for me to hear that these mountains are still growing upward as fast as our nails!

Captain James Cook named this area Doubtful Harbor in 1770. He was doubtful that once he would enter these waters, it would never get out again, given the many arms of this fjord. The Italian explorer Malaspina arrived in 1793, and his Spanish crew named a lot of the sites.

Doubtful Sound should really be called Doubtful Fjord. A fjord is a long, narrow inlet with steep sides or cliffs, created by glacial erosion, which is exactly what we have here. The word comes to English from Norwegian. I guess in New Zealand the word fjord never became popular, and I feel the name Doubtful Sound will remain for quite a bit longer.

Doubtful Sound is certainly a misnomer for another reason: there are very few if any sounds here. Silence reigns supreme. This is one of the world's most remote and magical places. The beauty and vastness takes my breath away. The cruise lasts an enchanting three hours, during which I mostly immerse my mind, and senses of smell, touch (my skin against pure air), and hearing in mother earth and father sky.

The tour gets us in many of the 'arms' of the fjord. One of the biggest is Crooked arm, which is 15 km (almost 10 miles) long. In the middle of it, while in front of a majestic view of mountains and water, the guide urges us to stop talking. The captain turns the engines off. There is complete silence. It feels like coming back to earth's origins. This is how grandiose earth must have felt to our ancestors millennia of years ago.

As the cruise continues, we get to the mouth of Doubtful Sound. The climate is colder, the wind stiffer, coming directly from the south west, from Antarctica. There are a few small islands as the land surrenders to the vast Tasman Sea. On top of one of them, dozens of fur seals are vegging out. I guess, for them, these overcast skies and cool air must feel like the tropics compared to the freezing waters they are used to swim in.

We see bottlenose dolphins coming back in the Sound, but not as well and as close as we did yesterday. Lastly, we spot the famous crested penguins, swimming just about fifty yards in front of our boat. It is rare, the guide says, to see this 'trifecta:' seals, dolphins, and penguins in the same boat trip. Once again, we luck out.

I venture to the outside decks of the boat several times to soak in the marvelous silence, the immensity of nature, in this remote area of enchanting wilderness. Tree avalanches are occasional vertical streaks of white pause in the vast green which dives into the deep blue.

We are extremely tired coming back. I doze off on the bus ride back, for five minutes, but that is a lot for someone like me who never learned, unfortunately, the art of the nap. As on our way in it was too cloudy, we stop briefly to see the view, but clouds within a minute cover the magnificent fjord again. Paola sleeps on last boat ride back.

In Manapouri, we board our trusted campervan and drive back towards Queenstown. In over 200 km, there is only one gas station. Thankfully, I pull in and they lady is still there, saying, "You must be a lucky person. I was supposed to leave at 6:30pm, but it got busy and I'm still here." I'm so happy to pay the NZ$79 for a full tank of gas. It's about 6:40pm on my watch. I would have probably had just about enough diesel to make it back to Queenstown from here – 115 kms - , but I'm glad I do not have to worry the whole way about running out of gas.

For tens of kilometers, once again, nothing, just beautiful hills and mountains and valleys. We do see lots of sheep, initially some deer clearly also being raised as livestock, and cows. One can reflect on the fact this is a land still sparsely populated. Just 700,000 Kiwis live in the South Island, which is the size of more than half of Italy, which in turn has over 60 millions inhabitants.

Once we get to Queenstown, we park near the Gondola, where we had previously spotted some free overnight on-street parking. I park so that the campervan does not stick out much in the road, a masterful move.

The apartment we had booked at Lomond Lodge is new, large, elegant, and Paola remarks that the kitchen is bigger than ours in Philadelphia. There is a huge window, floor to ceiling and as large as the whole wall, in the living room, looking over Queenstown below, which is glittering with activity, while here all is quiet. Another wonderful choice.

We immediately go out and walk three minutes downhill to the center of Queenstown. Our goal is clear and unanimous: a burger at Fergburger, the most famous eatery in town. The wait is only thirty minutes. We first go to get some milk at the supermarket, then Pietro and I wait outside Fergburger while Andrea and Paola go back to the apartment to get some fruit and water.

The few minutes Pietro and I wait alone are bliss, as we converse serenely, not only about the beautiful girls around us, but also about this wonderful trip and life in general. Pietro reveals that he has had a great time in New Zealand. I'm so happy!!

By the time Andrea and Paola are back, we have just picked up our four Fergburgers - two with the works for Paola and me, two more plain for Pietro and Andrea - , and two fries to share. We decide to go and devour them in the main square, along the bay, where we find an empty bench just big enough for the four of us.

The burgers are huge: Pietro finishes his first, Paola is a close second, Andrea a minute or two after her. I still have over a third left of mine! Pietro says I cannot let them down; he helps me by taking one bite out of my burger, the rest I slowly and methodically gulp down. It is soft, juicy, delicious. We also finish about 80% of our fries.

Then we walk around on the lake shore, noticing again how transparent and clean the water is. We have decided to also get ice cream. Paola and Andrea remember and spot a place close to us, practically on the side of the square along the bay.

I want to order the special 'Palomaki' (or some other similar name) Ice Cream Sundae, but they are out of it because they ran out of strawberries. I say they can substitute the strawberries with whatever else they want, but the staff, after checking with the kitchen, still says the Palomaki is out. Andrea and Pietro in the meanwhile order a cone with cookies and vanilla, and a cup of strawberry and lemon ice cream, respectively. I settle for the Banana Splurge, another NZ$10 Sundae.

The Banana Splurge is simply superb, one of the best ice creams I've ever had, really! It has some vanilla and also I think hazelnut ice cream, as well as macadamia nuts and other delights mixed inside. Paola, but especially I, devour it.

As we get back to our apartment, the weather is still pleasant. Another delightful part of this whole trip, now on its last night, is that we could always wear casual clothing. It was great. I must admit that I wore the same T-shirt and long sleeved polo two days in a row, which I never do, as the small luggage we brought did allow for a change of underwear every day, but not for enough shirts for every day. And that's ok once in a blue moon.

Sunday March 30

I go get breakfast for everyone. Once out of the apartment, I also pay for our stay. During our lavish morning meal in our vast kitchen and dining room, Andrea tries kiwiana! He is an adult finally! I call home, my dad answers. He is excited to hear lots of news regarding New Zealand, our trip, the sheep, the purity of this land. He says it'll be tough for him to get the New York Times, and look at my interview in the Science Tuesday section. I joke with him he should buy it at Oneglia, who manages the only store in his 800-people home town of Sant'Apollinare, in rural Abruzzo, Italy.

By about 10am, we get out of the apartment, right on schedule, and put our small overnight bags in the nearby campervan. My plan had been all along to get back on a mountain bike and ride down from the top of the Gondola ride. Paola Andrea and Pietro had planned to visit the Queenstown Garden. A happy compromise.

Excited as a little child with ice cream, I bike down the top of the Gondola again. Three exhilarating rides. My adrenaline level is at its highest. You could light a bulb with a drop of my blood! What fun! I once again manage never to fall down, and this time I do not even injure myself. Pure excitement.

On the way to the airport, I notice that there is a piece of paper on the far left side on the window wipers, on the windshield. Pietro pulls it out with his left hand as I pull over. It's a fine, for having illegally camped overnight. We decide to fight it right away, as we have proof we did not stay in the campervan that night. Eventually, it will be dropped, with just a polite email to the appropriate New Zealand authorities.

Before the airport, I also fill the tank with diesel. From the hotel to the campervan return site, Pietro is sitting in the front row giving me directions from the iPhone. It's wonderful to see him calm and collected contributing to the good outcome of this trip.

We return the campervan at Britz. We get charged another NZ$145 for the mileage (over 3,000 kms), which apparently has to do with the insurance we chose. Our rental agreement clearly says that the rate charges included unlimited mileage, as we show Sarah, the kind Britz agent. I'm a bit surprised, as this was the insurance the staff person at Christchurch had advised us to take. Thinking that I'm used to some overpaying when renting cars, I offer my credit card without fuss. It could have been worse with an over $1,300 campervan rental. They did not charge us for the bit of stove gas (1kg) we used.

The Queenstown airport is fairly new. We are booked for the 2:30pm Air New Zealand NZ644 flight from Queenstown to Auckland, where we are planned to arrive at 4:20pm. Our seats are 26A, 26B, 26C, and 25C – guess who gets this one?

We fly back now over the Remarkables mountain range. What a great name for these outstanding masses of rock. It's a bit sad to leave such a beautiful place, but so far from the rest of the world. The sadness comes from the fact that we may not come here again. I remember leaving beautiful Egypt, or Machu Picchu. Those are places which are great to visit once, but I had not wished strongly to move in and live there. I could certainly fancy to move to New Zealand, especially Queenstown, and live happily here.

In Auckland, we see many Maori at the airport. One group shouts loudly saying bye to relatives leaving the country. Everyone comes over to watch, and applauds. We spend the last NZ$45 cash we have: first for yogurt, Danishes, fruit salads and other food, and the last couple of dollars for chips.

Reflecting on the trip, I tell Paola I now really feel the world is small. After all, it only took about 12 hours from the west coast of the US to get to New Zealand. The world can be traveled all around, going anywhere. It only takes the will to do it.

The passport check-in here in Auckland is automatic. The most modern I've ever seen, in any continent. One scans his passport in a machine, and gets a ticket. With that ticket, one goes to a booth, where, inserting the ticket, lights come on with a sign in front saying, "Look straight here." Face recognition occurs in less than five seconds, and is followed by the gates opening.

Leaving this country, one can reflect that New Zealand, despite being so far from everything, has got the best of many things. They drive on the left, which is actually how driving was originally designed to be, going back to Ancient Rome. They use the metric system, as most of the world. Their houses are modern. One young guy going up the Gondola in Queenstown, a painter, told me the houses are supposed to 'let the outside in.' They have huge windows, lots of light, modern designs, cutting-edge technology inside.

Kiwis enjoy a socialized health system, so everyone can get basically free care everywhere, with short waits and very low deductibles. They pay five dollars for any prescriptions, no matter what the drug is. The doctors seemed professional, up-to-date, caring, and compassionate.

The best, of course, is their ecofriendly way of being. Everything is clean. The restaurant in Queenstown where we ate only sells food made within about 95 km (58 miles). New Zealanders try to eat what they make. The environment is uncontaminated, pristine. One feels like one could drink from their rivers, creeks, and lakes.

We take the 7:40pm Air New Zealand NZ6 from Auckland to Los Angeles. Happily, we are all together, even if in the back of the plane, in seats 57 D, E, F, G. We take off on time at about 8pm local time. We are supposed to land at 11:55am after a 12h15m flight, but the captain announces that flight time is about 11 hours and 20 minutes. We'll see.

Once again, there is a plug for recharging this MacBookAir, so I'm happy I can have ample time to record my fresh memories of this trip. I also do watch a romantic comedy. At around 10pm, I do manage to fall asleep, as Pietro and Andrea have already done, to my delight.

The flight is extremely bumpy, and at some point the bumpiest I've ever experienced, except may be the one time in Thailand. I pray, as usual. It's very cold, and so I start coughing, as I do when I'm cold. So I decide to wear the pillow case as a hat. I look ridiculous, I'm sure, but my head gets warmer.

I wake up at 4:52am, as the plane lights come on. We are already within about two hours of Los Angeles, about half way between Honolulu and LA on the flight map. We have crossed the International Time Zone again, so while we left around 8pm Auckland time on Sunday, after over 11 hours of flying we arrive at about 11am Los Angeles time, still on the same Sunday. Strange.

The first delayed plane of our all trip, would you believe it, is the last, US one. We are supposed to leave Los Angeles at 2:20pm on USAir 1926 and arrive in Philadelphia at 10:13pm after a 4 hour and 53 minutes flight. We have seats 12A,B, 13A,B. In the end, our delay will only be about an hour. Enough time to cast more great memories on paper.

Acknowledgements

Paola Luzi
Andrea P. Berghella
Pietro M. Berghella

www.ingramcontent.com/pod-product-compliance
Lightning Source LLC
Chambersburg PA
CBHW020521030426
42337CB00011B/502